THE JOURNEY OF THE PRODIGAL

From a Sot to a Saint

*The Amazing Transformation
of a Prodigal Boomer*

Tim Fortner

 **Eleos Press**

Cover Art and Design: Eleos Press
www.eleospress.com
Interior Formatting: Eleos Press
www.eleospress.com

All Scripture, unless otherwise noted, comes from the New International Version, Zondervan, and King James Version of the Holy Bible.

Also available in eBook form

ISBN-13: 978-1517003067

Sot:

One who is habitually drunk

Saint:

One who has been set apart; sanctified; made holy

"I went down on my knees a sot; I came up from them a saint."

Tim Fortner, September 16, 1977

Introduction

When I set out to write my story about a defining period in my life, I identified with the well-known parable of the prodigal son in Luke 15. The prodigal was the younger son who discovered his actions had consequences. Prodigal is an adjective which is defined as: "Recklessly spendthrift."[1] One who spends extravagantly until nothing is left. He was a foolish young man whose selfish ambition was to be independent of his father's rules and morality. Making one disastrous decision after another, he found himself as a servant to a citizen of the far country feeding his pigs. At this point he came to his senses.

I, too, was a foolish young man. I left home and left behind the teachings of my parents, grandparents, teachers and pastors. I discovered the disaster of self-centered living also.

I am writing my story not only as a legacy for my family, but also for the prodigals out there. My desire in telling my story is you might come to your senses and return home. For those who love prodigals, my desire is for my story to be one of encouragement—and give you hope.

Tim Fortner

---

[1] Merriam-Webster's Collegiate Dictionary.

DEDICATION

In memory of my parents, Bill and Johnnye Elizabeth Fortner. They gave me life, love, opportunities and an example to follow. I am glad they lived to see me get saved, sober and sane.

In memory of my in-laws, Houston and Hope Sipes. They gave me their daughter as my wife and a chance when I needed one.

To my wife, Gina, my life partner and the finest, most beautiful and thoughtful person I have ever known. She gave me hope and encouragement every step of the way. In many ways she is a prodigal herself, in that she loves recklessly, extravagantly and completely. Everything she does, she always does the best she possibly can, never any less. I love you more than you can imagine.

TABLE OF CONTENTS

STARTING OUT: THE JOURNEY BEGINS

"There was a man who had two sons. The younger one said to his father, 'Father, give me my share of the estate.' So he divided his property between them. Not long after that, the younger son got together all he had and set off for a distant country and there squandered his wealth in wild living. After he had spent everything, there was a severe famine in that whole country and he began to be in need" (Luke 15:11–14).

This is actually the third part of a three-part story. The first is the lost sheep; the second is the lost coin. The third story, however, is my story. I know what was going on in the mind of this younger son, for I, too, was the younger, prodigal son. This young man, not much more than a boy, wanted to be out from under the restraint of his father's rules. Did you notice how impatient he was to be gone? We read that not long after receiving his portion he got together all he had and set off for the distant country. He did not leave anything behind. He then set about wasting his wealth in wild living. He spent everything. This young man did not save a single penny. Impatient to be gone from his father's house and rules, he was just as impulsive with his money.

It is interesting to note in the first two situations, the shepherd goes to search for the lost sheep and the woman searches diligently for the lost coin, resulting in both finding what they were searching for. In the young man's situation, the father does not go searching for the young man. Why? The wise father knew the prodigal must want to return. To go after him and bring him home would not solve the problem. The prodigal had to discover some truths about himself and life. Most businesses, schools, and churches have a lost and found department. When we lose something, we usually start a search by going back to the last place we remember having it.

In his search for what he lost, the prodigal son discovers some important truths about life. The prodigal had to recognize his own sin, his own wrong choices. No excuses. Here are the first essential truths: Sin will take you further than you want to go. Sin will keep you longer than you want to stay. Sin will cost you more than you want to pay. How long did it take the prodigal to realize these truths? We're not sure, but in my case, it took five years to waste all my father had given me. I went off to the "far country" (college) in 1963. In the next five years I was expelled from two different institutions four times. The money was gone, wasted in wild living with nothing to show for it. Return home then, right?

No, neither I nor the prodigal son had yet come to our senses.

In the parable we read there came a great famine. The young man was hungry. I, too, was hungry for something in my life, something that would fill the void which my wild living had not filled. In fact, the void seemed to be even worse than before. The prodigal in our story stayed in the far country, finding a job, but not finding what would fill his longing for something he knew was missing. Have you known such emptiness in your life? I have. Rebellion always causes famine. Did you notice the prodigal longed to fill his stomach? He longed to have a life with meaning. I had squandered my opportunities for an education to prepare me for life.

WHAT ARE YOU SEEKING?

In the Gospel of John, the Apostle writes about the first day he met Jesus. John and Andrew were young men who had been under the teaching of John the Baptist. John the Baptist pointed out Jesus to them the day after Jesus' baptism and told them: "Look, the Lamb of God!" (John 1:36). The two young men immediately turned around and followed Jesus. When Jesus saw them following, He asked them, "What do you seek?" (John 1:38)

Let me ask you the following questions which we all have asked ourselves before:

- What are you looking for in life?
- What are you seeking?
- Where are you looking?
- What have you found?
- How has it impacted your life?
- What is holding you back?
- When are you going to do something about what is holding you back?
- How long did the prodigal stay in the far - country?

We are not given this information. I know I stayed in the far country and away from my father's house for fourteen long years. Let me share my story with you.

What was it the young man in this story and I were looking for? We were looking to have fun and to live the way we wanted to live: drinking, partying, wild living. It was the 1960s, we thought we had discovered the real joys of life. We would explore life and live it to its fullest. Living in the far country was simply living the way we wanted to live without anyone forcing their rules upon us.

My parents left me at Murray State College in Murray, Kentucky, on a Sunday afternoon in September 1963. Having unpacked all my belongings, my mother made up my bed as she had done so many times before. My father talked to me about balancing my checkbook. They both talked about studying and going to class.

On that very Sunday night, my first night in the far country, my childhood friend Max Lewis and I found where to get some liquor and got drunk. Coming in late to the freshman dorm, we were stopped by the campus police. They gave us a stern warning about drinking, took our new school IDs, and told us to see the dorm monitor the next day. I was discovering that there are always those in authority whose purpose is to enforce the laws and rules for rebels such as myself. A pattern was being established. Priorities were being set in place.

In each person's life, there is always one thing more important than other things. This one thing becomes our passion, and we spend our time and efforts pursuing this passion. It creates a domino effect, and everything will fall into place from the one thing we pursue. It is the same principle of sowing and reaping: you reap what you sow and you always reap more than you sow and later than you sow. The consequences of my pursuing this one thing—wild living—would cause other things to fall into my life: expulsion from school, lost opportunities, becoming an alcoholic, DUIs, and several nights in jail. Car wrecks and heartaches and sleepless nights for my parents.

I can see the prodigal's father coming to the place each day where he last saw his son before he disappeared around the bend in the road. With tears in his eyes and longing in his heart, he lifted up prayer after desperate prayer to heaven for the prodigal's return. Day after day, week after week, month after month, year after year, he waited and he prayed.

In 1968, after my fourth expulsion from college, I knew a degree was not in the cards for me. I was working, I was drinking, and I was beginning to realize I needed to do something about my life. I was a twenty-three-year-old with nothing to show for my life up to this point. I needed to change. I needed to grow up. I wondered, *"What do grownups do?"* I knew they marry and have families. This would be my direction. I was looking at the route others had followed, and I decided to follow that route.

So I married a young woman I had dated in college. Our marriage was in trouble almost immediately. My drinking was out of control, and my life was unmanageable. Next solution? Have a child.

"Being a husband had not worked," I reasoned. "Maybe being a father would."

What was I looking for? I had always looked for one thing—to be happy. Where was I looking? In partying, living life the way I wanted to live it. When that backfired, I looked for relationships that would change me and make me happy and fulfilled—to become a husband and father, to have a job and settle down. What did I find? I was emptier than ever before and had brought more heartache to more people than before. What was holding me back? Lack of education. But lack of education had really been my fault due to my drinking. I had to cut back on the drinking. It didn't happen.

It was 1973 and my ten-year high school reunion was coming up. I was now divorced, unemployed, an alcoholic, and an absentee father. I didn't want to go to my reunion. I was a failure, and I knew it. Now everyone else would recognize my failure. In the end, I got drunk and went to the reunion.

I remembered the last day we met as a senior class in May 1963. The president of our class, Jimmy Milligan, said we needed to vote on when we would have our first reunion. The options were in ten years or twenty years. I remember laughing with my classmates as we tried to imagine ten or twenty years in the future. It seemed impossibly far away. We voted on ten years.

On a May evening in 1963, I had walked across the stage in the auditorium of Peabody High

School, in Trenton, Tennessee, to receive my diploma from our principal and family friend, John Underwood. I did not know how fast the next ten years would pass; I did not know I would never see some of my classmates and teachers again; I did not know how important the next ten years were going to be. The "domino effect" was about to start, and the things which would fall into my life were inevitable given the choices I would make.

Signs

When indoor malls became popular and each seemed to get bigger and bigger, the malls placed signs which read, "You Are Here." At my tenth reunion, I began to realize where I was. While talking to my classmates, those childhood friends I had grown up with, I realized they were becoming responsible adults. They had jobs as teachers, lawyers, engineers, salesmen, farmers, or factory workers. They had spouses, homes, and children. My classmates showed me what life was supposed to be about. They were living it; I was not.

In a way I can look back now and see it was a turning point. All the signs pointed to the prodigal's pig pen, and I knew YOU ARE HERE. I began to desire to change my life more than ever before. I began to look back at the paths I had chosen and the results of my choices. My decision to drink and party had been disastrous. My life was falling into a pattern that many alcoholics have experienced: the circle of defeat, depression, and despair.

Looking back to my childhood days, the sign we often see in neighborhoods comes to mind: SLOW DOWN: CHILDREN AT PLAY. Growing up in Trenton, a small West Tennessee town of 4,500, in the 1950s and 1960s seemed the ideal life in the twentieth century. Trenton could have served as the set for Frank Capra's, "It's a Wonderful Life." Three main streets, High Street, College, and Church led to a downtown with a court square with a fountain, a statue of Davy Crockett, and a majestic court house.

The court square was surrounded by locally owned businesses. This was before the time of the national retailers and big-box stores and malls. We had three local banks, three locally owned drug stores, complete with soda fountains, furniture stores, hardware stores, barber shops, and cafes. One did business with people who knew you and your family. My father, Bill Fortner, was an optometrist. My mother, Johnye Elizabeth Fortner, was an English teacher. We were your typical family, living in the most optimistic period of the twentieth century. Having survived a horrendous depression in which famine was a problem, and having successfully fought a World War, we were a nation fully prepared and ready to live life.

Looking back historically, I wonder if we had been a "prodigal nation" that had to experience famine and war to bring us back to our forefathers' dream of one nation under God. As a result, we were a nation ready to go to work. Worship, work, and respect for authority were the rules of the land, and so began a time of the "Baby Boom," an optimistic time of opportunity and old-time values that hearkened back to the days of our Puritan and Pilgrim founders.

My brother Phil was born in 1943, I arrived in 1945, and my little sister, Nancy, completed our family by being born on Mother's Day in 1949. Today we all look back to the era we grew up and realize how fortunate we were. My brother would become an optometrist, taking over our father's practice he had started in the early 1940s. My sister followed our mother and became an English teacher, as well as a prolific writer. I ended up in the optical industry as a speaker and teacher.

I am glad we slow down for children at play. Such a carefree time of life should go slowly. It was a time when summer days and nights were special, a time for catching fireflies in jars, playing hide-and-seek, riding bikes with friends, going fishing, camping out, and taking family vacations. Television was a wonder. We only had three channels and no remote control—except my brother and me. We watched television as a family. No profanity, no sex, no nudity. It was at time and place of perpetual sunshine and wonder. We enjoyed wholesome entertainment which upheld traditional values. Good always prevailed, evil never did. We laughed and we cried, but we were never embarrassed by the content of the entertainment. I still enjoy watching Andy Griffith as Sheriff Andy Taylor and Don Knotts as Barney Fife. It was a time filled with the wonder and awe of childhood.

I realized I was no longer a child at play. I needed to put away childish things. Stop signs are common on our streets. Stop means to come to a complete stop—not a rolling stop—and look both ways. Stop signs occur at crossroads and intersections. This is true in life also. God gave us instructions regarding crossroads: "Stand at the crossroads and look; ask for the ancient paths, ask where the good way is, and walk in it, and you will find rest for your souls. But you said, 'We will not walk in it.' I appointed watchmen over you and said, 'Listen to the sound of the trumpet!' But you said, 'We will not listen'" (Jeremiah 6:16-17).

You understand the crossroads we encounter, don't you? They occur when the pursuit of happiness intersects with the pursuit of truth. The two ways are distinctly marked. One is the narrow way and entered by the straight gate. The other is the broad way, entered by the wide gate. I made a rolling stop, and I did not ask which is the best way to go. I had watchmen over me—my loving parents—but I would not listen and I would not walk in the narrow way. I chose the broad way and entered the way which seemed right to me but would lead to destruction. The dominoes of consequences fell into place and created problem after problem.

I was searching for something to satisfy me. So far in my journey I had found I was headed down a wrong path. I made a wrong turn, and I needed to turn around, change direction. Have you ever stopped some place and asked for directions? Often you get a long, drawn-out list of turns and landmarks to take you to where you are going, but you cannot follow them accurately. You end up more lost and further away than when you first started. The best possible solution is to follow a person who knows the way. It would be even better if the person would get in the car with you and will tell you which way to turn. I needed somebody to come into my life and tell me which way I needed to go.

We all have to figure out what we are looking for in the first place. The prodigal and I were looking for the same thing. We wanted to be happy and to be satisfied. I could really identify with the Rolling Stones biggest hit, "(I Can't Get No) Satisfaction." Their lyrics were mine—"I try and I try and I try"—but I could not seem to find this elusive something that would satisfy. I wanted satisfaction; I wanted rest for my soul

The prodigal in our story must have realized he was in trouble when he found himself broke. He was broke, but not yet broken. What did he do? He hired himself out to a citizen of that far country. He settled down to try and find a life in the far country. This would be his life—a life in which many of us found ourselves trapped in and by. We could observe others going on with their lives in the right way. It seemed we were on a parallel path, searching for the same things but headed in the opposite direction.

The night of my tenth reunion, many of my classmates were headed in the right direction. It was as if I could observe them headed down Interstate 40 traveling east, while I was just a short distance away, headed west. I did not understand what I was doing and why I could not get turned around. Every time I wanted to do good—to quit drinking, to get my life in order—I found myself drinking again and doing what

I did not want to do. The Apostle Paul was right in Romans 7:24 when he described himself as "wretched." I was sick and tired of being sick and tired.

I was getting closer to the truth. I was searching for the way back. But there was a sign I had not heeded yet, the one it took me four more years to obey. It is a triangular sign in bold yellow with black print: YIELD.

Beverly Sills, the opera diva, had it right when she said, "There are no shortcuts to anyplace worth going." I was about to find there were no shortcuts. I would have to go back to where I made the wrong turn and start over the right way. But I was not there yet.

The Signs of Alcoholism or Problem Drinking[2]

1. Have you ever decided to stop drinking for a week or so, but only lasted for a couple of days? __ Yes __No
2. Do you wish people would mind their own business about your drinking—stop telling you what to do? __Yes __No
3. Have you ever switched from one kind of drink to another in hope that this would keep you from getting drunk? __Yes __No

---

[2] Copyright@1973 by A.A. World Services, Inc.

4. Have you had to have an "eye-opener" upon awakening during the past year? __Yes __No
5. Do you envy people who can drink without getting into trouble? __Yes __No
6. Have you had problems connected with drinking during the past year? __Yes __ No
7. Has your drinking caused trouble at home? __Yes __ No
8. Do you ever try to get "extra" drinks at a party because you do not get enough? __Yes __No
9. Do you tell yourself you can quit drinking any time you want to, even though you keep getting drunk when you don't mean to? __Yes __No
10. Have you missed days of work or school because of drinking? __Yes __No
11. Do you have "blackouts?" __Yes __No
12. Have you ever felt that your life would be better if you did not drink? __Yes __No

Did you answer "Yes" four or more times? If so, these are *signs you may be a problem drinker.*

The prodigal and I set out to do one thing: to enjoy life on our terms. We were both convinced our father's way of enjoying life was not the best way. We were both discovering we were wrong, but we were looking for alternative routes and shortcuts.

We both were looking to see if we could stay in the far country and find the satisfaction we were looking for in life. We were not quite ready to return to our fathers' rules and ways.

SOUVENIRS AND MEMENTOS

Have you seen the T-shirt that says, "Been There, Done That, Bought the T-shirt?" We have all acquired things from trips, vacations and journeys. Souvenirs and mementos remind us of a vacation or trip. There are also photographs which show us standing in front of landmarks, beaches, mountains, and famous places. And of course we all have memories.

Family vacations when I was growing up consisted of going to Florida to stay at Stella's Apartments on the beach outside Panama City. I have one photograph from that era in the 1950s I cherish to this day. It is a black-and-white photograph with my father. He has his arm around my shoulders, and I have my arm around his waist. He was thirty-nine years old and I was twelve years old. I had not yet entered those dreaded teenage years, and I really enjoyed being with my family on our annual summer vacation.

We were often joined by the Underwood family. Mr. Underwood was the principal of our high school; he and his wife Grace had four daughters. We enjoyed those trips, laughing, swimming in the Gulf of Mexico, fishing, eating, and just being together.

The photos and mementos I gathered from those days are still cherished memories of days gone by. What mementos did the prodigal and I collect from our years in the "far country?" Destructive habits that took away opportunities. Loss of material goods. Loss of respect for ourselves. Our souvenirs are like scars from the collisions we had with loved ones, authorities, and life in general. Life in the fast lane on the broad way is dangerous.

The first time I was expelled from college was 1965; I was nineteen years old. I left school and went to Florida with two of my college friends who had also been expelled. We found work as painters. We lived in a two-room apartment where I slept on a sofa. We sent postcards back to our friends in college showing the beach, palm trees, and sunny skies. The truth is, I was miserable and homesick. On more than one occasion, I cried myself to sleep.

I know the prodigal son is a fictional character in a parable told by the Lord Jesus, but I bet Jesus knew someone exactly like him. Prodigals have always been there, and they are all around us today, searching for something to make life worth living. Prodigals cry themselves to sleep at night, shedding tears of homesickness, tears for mistakes made, and tears for the consequences of wrong choices. No wonder we prodigals drink and take drugs to deaden the pain.

Our T-shirts might read, "Been There, Done That, Wish I Hadn't!" Our post cards never say, "Wish you were here!"; they read "Don't come here!"

THE JOURNEY OF THE PRODIGAL

Our souvenirs are scars: physical, mental and emotional.

We never stopped and asked for directions. We should have talked with someone who had been here before, but it seems we cannot learn from our wrong choices. Our decision making is flawed. My trip to Florida in 1965 was a miserable time in my life. It was the first time I began to realize I had made a serious wrong turn. If I could have gone back, I would not make the same mistakes, but as I said, I had not heeded the one sign with its command to yield.

I came back from Florida in the spring of 1965, worked at Horace May's Texaco Service Station for a couple of months, and got back in school at Murray State. I had learned my lesson, right? Wrong! Prodigals are hardheaded or, at least, I was. Probably the prodigal in our story was also. After all, when he ended up broke, common sense would have told him he needed to return home. Yet he went to work in the far country. He had not hit bottom yet, as they like to say in AA.

So I had been there, bought the T-shirt, and experienced the consequences of my wrong choices. Now I would make right choices. The only problem was, I had not and would not give up drinking. I thought I could be a successful student and continue to party also. I could manage this now. I hadn't learned you cannot serve two masters. I was running a race, but as the Apostle Paul asked the Galatians, "You were running a good race. Who cut in on you?"

(Galatians 5:7). I was always running but never finishing the race, ever learning but never coming to the truth.

It took less than a week in the summer of 1965 for me to be arrested for a DUI and expelled from college again. Horrified at my unbelievable stupidity, I realized I was at risk for being drafted into the military during the Vietnam War. Fortunately, I was able to get into Lambuth College in Jackson, Tennessee.

Here is where it gets even more confusing. I did well in school for the next year, making good grades; I was even initiated into a fraternity. I believed I had arrived where I was supposed to be. But the prodigal is not an easy person to understand, even though they are often easy to love. By the fall of 1966, I had quit going to class and was drinking every day. Expelled once again, I went back to Florida. I realize now, as a parent, that I had made my parents' life a nightmare.

I received one more opportunity in 1967 to return to Lambuth, only to be expelled once again. How could this be? I was an alcoholic, and I could not stay sober. As I already explained, I further compounded my troubles by getting married and having a son in the next two years. By 1973, my marriage fell apart due to my drinking.

Here is where I will continue my story. Having viewed my scrapbook of mementos, souvenirs, and photographs from 1963 to 1973, I'll share what happened next.

THE JOURNEY OF THE PRODIGAL

Watching a prodigal is much like watching a tightrope walker walk on a thin wire, hundreds of feet above the ground with no safety net. We hold our breath as he sways back and forth and wonder whether he will make it to the safety of the other side. Would I make it? Would I fall? Would I be able to go on if I fell again?

THE REST STOP

"My candle burns at both ends; it will not last the night; but ah, my foes, and oh, my friends—It gives a brilliant light!"[3]

I was burning out. Nonstop drinking made me realize my life was headed to a dead end. The moment of realization I experienced at my tenth reunion caused me to re-evaluate my life up to that point. I was horrified to have wasted ten of my most important and precious years.

I pulled over for a rest stop. My engine was overheating, I was running low on fuel, and I was headed nowhere. I began to look at my life. It was a nightmare. Alcohol was a problem a big problem that needed to be managed. I needed a new philosophy: "eat, drink and be merry" was not working. I was weary and burdened and in need of a truth that would guide me and set me on the right course. Looking back, I saw how the domino effect can be disastrous when the one thing you pursue is the wrong thing. Make one bad choice causes a ripple effect as one bad thing after another happens.

Where would I look for the truth? In a book store, I visited the self-help area filled with books on how to succeed, how to think and grow rich, how to plan your work and work your plan, how to develop

---

[3] Edna St. Vincent Millay, who died at age 58

the habits of excellence. All I had to do was work hard, think positively, and take a humanistic approach to tapping into the power within. I bought into these ideas because they sounded right, and some truths that some they taught were true. (I later would discover why this was so.) Some were half-truths, and some were out-and-out lies.

I took a job as a retail clerk in a shoe store, working six days a week for not very much money. However, I found I enjoyed getting up each day and earning a paycheck every week. I worked hard and did my best—nothing wrong with that—and soon I was offered my dream job as a salesman for an optical laboratory. Good salary. Benefits. Company car. Wow! I was on my way!

I did not quit drinking during this period, but I had curbed my drinking during the work week and partied on the weekend. I showed up for work every day and did the best I could. The great thing about my new job was that drinking with clients, doctors, and entertaining at conventions was part of my job description—or so I reasoned. My boss and the other salesmen all did this, so since I was already an experienced drinker, this was fine with me.

Life was good in 1974. I was finally making some headway and succeeding at my job. I enjoyed the industry I was in and the customers I called on in Kentucky, Tennessee and Mississippi. Did I drink too much sometimes? Yes, but it was not as bad as before and I was in control—or so I thought.

THE JOURNEY OF THE PRODIGAL

In 1975, I met a beautiful young nursing student, Gina Sipes. I believe I fell in love with her almost immediately. I had never been this happy before. Our courtship and falling in love were like something out of a movie. We danced the nights away, drank, and partied, but knew we had to be about our business the next day. She was never much of a drinker, and like many alcoholics, I had such a high tolerance, I seemed to have the proverbial "hollow leg." Things were not what they seemed.

Gina and I were married on June 4, 1976. She had another year in nursing school. I was an ambitious young salesman, 30 years old, climbing the ladder of success. The rest stop was over. It had accomplished its purpose. I was on track now. I changed jobs for a better paying job in the optical industry at the same time Gina discovered she was pregnant. Our daughter, Carrie Tobin Fortner, arrived on May 3, 1977, just in time for her mother's graduation from nursing school.

I wanted more than ever to be a good husband and good father. But I had yet to come to understand the meaning of the sign that kept telling me to YIELD!

THE SUMMER OF 1977

I will never forget the summer of 1977. I had changed positions a couple of times in the last year and now had a frame line and a territory which included several states in the Southeast. Gina was working as a nurse, and Carrie was a joy and delight. I now had an infant daughter and my seven-year-old son, Robert, from my first marriage.

I was thirty-one years old, and I knew I had a problem, a secret that was killing me and was going to ruin my life. I was an alcoholic. My drinking was worse than it had ever been. I wanted more than anything in my life to be sober, but for the life of me I could not stay sober.

My self-help philosophy was empty and useless. I would leave our apartment on Monday morning, sometimes having to drive for hundreds of miles. Trying to convince myself I would not take a drink, I would repeat to myself over and over, "I will not take a drink! I will not take a drink!" When I arrived at my destination, I'd find the closest bar and begin to drink until I was drunk. I was experiencing blackouts and was unable to remember what I had done, where I was, or what day of the week it was. I was trying to move a mountain—a problem with alcohol—that loomed over my life, but try as I might, I could not move past it.

The summer of 1977 was the most horrific summer of my life. Each day I lost a little more hope that I would ever get sober and be successful at anything. I knew I would be fired from my job. I knew Gina would not want to raise a daughter in the home of an alcoholic. To avoid my boss, I took the phone off the hook when I got home on Fridays and would not put it back until I left on Monday. I was running out of time and hope. A normal life seemed impossible.

Have you ever been hopeless? I have. It is a condition many a prodigal has experienced. It is one of the most devastating emotions one can experience. We know physically we need, oxygen, water and food to survive—in that order. We can go weeks without food, days without water, but only minutes without oxygen. Hope is the oxygen of our souls; without it we die.

Want to know why so many prodigals take their lives? They run out of hope and they cannot survive without it. Want to know why so many prodigals are alcoholics and drug abusers? Because they are trying to dull the pain of hopelessness.

So it was on that fateful day, September 16, 1977, when this prodigal came to the decision to end his life. I could not live this way any longer. Death was preferable to living a life without any hope of getting better.

THE JOURNEY OF THE PRODIGAL

I was staying at a Holiday Inn on West End Avenue in Nashville. I awoke on Friday morning with all of the usual hangover symptoms: throbbing headache, dry mouth, shaky hands, bleary eyes. It was a hangover like no other I had experienced. Looking back, I realize the cause. The last domino in a long line of falling dominoes since 1963 had fallen. I was out of hope. Complete hopelessness was hanging over me. What a dark place! What a scary sensation! I could look back and see the long line of broken promises, ruined dreams, and wrong turns. It was the end of the line.

I looked in the mirror at the thirty-one-year-old man I had become. A prodigal in a pig pen. Death would be a relief. I stepped out on the balcony of my tenth-floor room. The memories of that morning are as fresh to me today as they were almost four decades ago. It was a beautiful fall day. (Officially it was the still summer, but fall was just around the corner). The skies were autumn blue with no clouds. It was cool morning with a feel of fall in the air, complete with a touch of color in the foliage.

I put my left foot on the bottom rail. I had not put my shoes on yet and can, to this day, remember how the rail felt in the arch of my left foot. I put my right leg over the railing and began to push up with my left foot. I thought of Gina and how this would impact her life. I knew my infant daughter would never remember me and my seven-year-old son, only faintly. My mother and father would be crushed, as would my brother and sister. A great, loud and deep sob came out of the depths of my being. I was crushed under the weight of hopelessness.

I do not know how close I was to reaching the point of no return when my weight would shift and I would plunge to my death ten floors below. I do remember my heart racing and my hair standing up on my neck. I was scared to death and scared of death.

At the last moment I pushed back and fell on my knees in my hotel room. I pulled the heavy red and gold bed cover up to my face and prayed. I still remember the exact words: "Lord Jesus, *if you are real,* come into this room and into my heart and save me—or else I will die!"

Did you notice the little word *if? If* is probably the biggest little word in the English language. *If* denotes an element of doubt. But here is the key: Are you an honest doubter, one who is honestly seeking the truth? If you are, then ask and you shall receive. Something happened to me on September 16, 1977. Different people experience this moment we call salvation in different ways. I experienced a calmness and a peace. My mind, though in a fog of alcohol, had enough clarity to call Alcoholics Anonymous for the first time in my life. What followed next was not a coincidence. The domino effect was about to begin, for I had put in place the right domino of priority. I soon discovered my problem was not my problem. My priority was my problem.

I decided it was time to obey the sign: YIELD.

I might also add that I now wanted to obey another sign: NO U TURNS!

ARE WE THERE YET?

Almost there.

"When [the prodigal] came to his senses, he said: 'How many of my father's hired men have food to spare, and here I am starving to death! I will set out [arise] and go back to my father and say to him: Father, I have sinned against heaven and you. I am no longer worthy to be called your son; make me like one of your hired men.' So he got up and went to his father " (Luke 15:17-20).

When I called AA that morning, I discovered everything was lining up in place. First, an AA meeting was taking place in just moments and only blocks away from my hotel. I arrived and entered a new world where I would find people like myself, prodigals who spent years in the far country. Prodigals who had made wrong turns like I had made. People who had been where I had been and had turned around and headed back in the right direction. People who had lost all hope and found it again—a hope that does not disappoint.

I listened to the speaker and the comments made by other attendees. "One day at a time," I heard them say more than once. "Let go and let God"—whatever that meant. It all seemed too trite to be of any help. Once again, when one finds the one thing they are supposed to do, everything begins to fall in place. As the meeting was ending, a well-dressed businessman came up to me and asked, "Do you need some help?" He was my good Samaritan, my guardian angel sent to me as sure as the flaky, second-class angel, Clarence Oddbody was sent to George Bailey in *It's a Wonderful Life.*

I do not remember his name, only that he was a vice president of an insurance agency. He took me to his office and told his secretary to hold his calls. Closing the office door behind him, he sat down at his desk and began to talk to me. He told me his story of how he had wandered down the same road I had and ended up in a pig pen, just like I had. He asked me my wife's name, my home phone, where I lived and worked. Then before I knew it, he picked up the phone and called Gina. He handed the phone to me and I heard Gina say hello.

For the second time that morning, I was scared to death, but all of a sudden everything came rushing out of me. There it is again: *When the one thing is the right thing, it sets in motion a chain reaction where everything begins to fall in place.* The words came rushing out, as if I did not say it quickly, I would somehow begin to rationalize it. "I am an alcoholic," I confessed. "I cannot stay sober." I began to tell her about my day. I could not imagine what was going through her mind. She later told me she was frightened. Married only 15 months, a new mother with a three-month-old child, living in a two-bedroom apartment—it would have been overwhelming for anyone. On this day, I discovered not only had I married a beautiful, warm, intelligent woman, but I had also found a faithful partner for life. "I will come get you right away," she offered. "I can drive home," I told her. Her response took away my greatest fear. All the other fears and troubles I had imagined continued to topple. I also made another great discovery that day: The truth will set you free.

I was headed for home. For the first time in fourteen years I was headed in the right direction, and look who was waiting for me, someone I had not been on speaking terms with since I left home. My heavenly Father was waiting for me, His eyes on the bend in the road where He last saw me.

"But while [the prodigal] was a long way off, his father saw him and was filled with compassion for him; he ran to his son, threw his arms around him and kissed him" (Luke 15:20).

I do not remember the drive home to Jackson. I am not sure what Gina and I talked about that first night. I do know the next morning, I called my boss and told him what was going on with me and apologized for my behavior. I expected to be fired, but he simply said, "Are you ready to go to work now?" "Yes, sir, I am," I replied. The dominos were toppling, one by one.

I began attending AA meetings each week. I found a group and a sponsor and began to work the program. The first step was to admit I was an alcoholic, I was powerless over alcohol, and my life had become unmanageable. I did not have the power to overcome my compulsion to drink. I was powerless. Overcoming was as impossible for me as pushing over Mount Everest.

The next step was believing that a Power greater than myself could restore me to sanity. I then made a decision to turn my will and my life over to the care of God as I came to understand Him. God became my priority, first in my life.

I now was headed in the right direction. Gina watched nervously to see if the change was real or not. It took a season of sobriety before she could say to people, "I have a new husband!"

Nobody wanted me to come back home more than my Heavenly Father, as illustrated by the prodigal's father in this parable. I can picture the prodigal that day. His fine wardrobe had been reduced to rags, and his hair was in disarray. He was a gaunt figure coming down the road that day. There was no bounce in his step like the day he left. His slow steps suggested how weak and hungry he was.

"The son said to him, 'Father, I have sinned against heaven and against you. I am no longer worthy to be called your son.' But the father said to his servants, 'Quick, bring the best robe and put it on him. Put a ring on his finger and sandals on his feet. Bring the fattened calf and kill it. Let's have a feast and celebrate. For this son of mine was dead and is alive again; he was lost and is found.' So they began to celebrate" (Luke 15:21-24).

The prodigal and I had discovered some truths which enabled us to start over.

We learned the truth about sin.

We finally woke up to the truth that living in sin is contrary to our Father's will and leads to destruction. Father always knows best.

We came to loathe what we once loved. The wise Father actually allowed the sin to drive us back home to Him.

The prodigal and I finally came to realize we could start over. We learned the one thing we must do—we must return to our Father's house. "Seek ye first the kingdom of God and His righteousness and all the things you need He will provide" (Matthew 6:33)

The prodigal and I both learned what we were looking for: the peace that passes understanding. We also learned where to look: "Come unto me all you who are weary and heavy laden and I will give you rest" (Matthew 11:28).

We knew what we had found. We had found what our hearts had always wanted. Satisfaction. Peace. Rest. We discovered where it had always been in my Father's house. "One thing I have desired of the Lord, this is what I will seek that I might dwell in the house of the Lord all the days of my life" (Psalm 27)

Do you realize there can be only one thing that is the most important thing in your life? You must ask yourself this question: What is the most important thing in my life?

Let me assure you, based on the lesson, every prodigal who makes it back can tell you: If the Lord Jesus Christ is the most important thing in our life, it will create the right domino effect. How do I mean this? It's simple. When the most important thing in your life is the right thing, then when it is set in motion, everything else will fall into place.

Are you searching for the most important thing, the one thing that is most needed? Martha was upset because she was doing all the work in the kitchen while her sister, Mary, sat at the feet of Jesus, listening to Him. Consider what Jesus spoke to Martha in Luke 10:41, "Martha, Martha, you are worried about many things. One thing is needful and Mary has done it." Are you worrying about too many things? Got problems? No problem is too big for the Lord. With God, nothing is impossible.

Turn around. Start back. It is never too late to do the right thing!

A New Road Map: A New Way

     Life was beginning to make sense for the first time in a long time. I remember coming home with my Alcoholics Anonymous' "Big Book" and sharing the twelve steps of AA with Gina. "This is scriptural," she remarked. "This is the plan of salvation." I began to read the Bible, and now I had two self-help books to help me understand life. What I had discovered was a new road map leading me to live my life in a new way. It is interesting to note that in the early days of Christianity, Christians and their beliefs were called, "The Way."

     For the first time in over a decade I opened the Word of God and began to read it. Between reading the Bible and AA materials, I found the common denominators and recognized the pattern. The pattern is always sequential. Cause and effect. Sow and reap. We refer to the chain reaction as the "domino effect," the phrase that illustrates the cascading, far-reaching effects of a certain action.

     Let me share with you the Twelve Steps of Alcoholics Anonymous. Notice they are numbered in a sequence, for there is a priority of first things first. When I began to work the Twelve Steps, I asked my sponsor what I would do when I finished the steps. He smiled and said, "You never finish them. You keep working them as long as you live." I learned your passions lead you to practice your passion, and your practice leads to development of greater skills, and greater skills lead to greater results, and greater results lead to great enjoyment and greater passion. I was learning how to stay sober one day at a time. When I received my "chip," recognizing thirty consecutive days of sobriety, I was thrilled with my success. I was beginning a life of sobriety, one day at time, by working the twelve steps.

The 12 Steps of AA

1. We admitted we were powerless over alcohol, that our lives had become unmanageable.
2. Came to believe that a Power greater than ourselves could restore us to sanity.
3. Made a decision to turn our will and our lives over to the care of God as we understood Him.
4. Made a searching and fearless moral inventory of ourselves.
5. Admitted to God, to ourselves, and to another human being the exact nature of our wrongs.
6. Were entirely ready to have God remove all these defects of character.
7. Humbly ask Him to remove our shortcomings.
8. Made a list of all persons we had harmed, and became willing to make amends to them all.
9. Made direct amends to such people wherever possible, except when to do so would injure them or others.

10. Continued to take personal inventory and, when we were wrong, promptly admitted it.
11. Sought through prayer and meditation to improve our conscious contact with God as we understood Him, praying for knowledge of His will for us and the power to carry it out.
12. Having had a spiritual awakening as the result of these steps, we tried to carry this message to others, and to practice these principles in all our affairs.

Now as I was studying Scripture at the same time and, with my wife's help as she pointed them out, I discovered the similarities. The first step is to recognize we are powerless over sin. Drunkenness is a sin. Now, I am not disputing that both AA and the American Medical Association refer to alcoholism as a disease. I would just add this: Alcoholism is a disease as is all sin, and the wages of sin is death. I was at death's door on September 16, 1977.

The first step was to recognize I was powerless over my drinking. I already knew that. Fourteen years of nonstop drinking and all my futile efforts to stop had convinced me of this truth. The lie of the self-help books was I had the power within me to overcome this problem. Try and try as I might, I could not find the power. Alcohol was my personal demon, described as cunning and baffling. I had made alcohol and drinking a part of my life, and it had become a priority. The evidence was overwhelming, and the verdict was clear: My life was unmanageable.

The first step came to me in desperation and fear for my very life. In my hotel room on September 16, 1977, I knew the sequence of dominoes had come to the end of the line. My only option was to continue to live life this way, and it was too painful. Hopeless of ever getting sober, I came within inches of throwing my life away. Looking back at the tangled disarray of my life, I saw the toppled dominoes of empty promises and dreams I had dreamed when I was young. This only made me realize I would never overcome this problem in my own power.

Step two follows. A ray of hope broke through like a ray of light to a miner trapped in a cave-in, a miry pit with oxygen running out. I came to believe in a Power, God Almighty, greater than myself and greater than my problem, who could restore me to sanity. Like a trapped miner I looked desperately for a light from above. Pushing back from that balcony on that fateful morning was the beginning of a new sequence, a new order in my life, a new way. I went down on my knees that morning as a sot, and I know now I came up from my knees a saint. The prayer I prayed on that morning almost forty years ago was the prayer of an honest doubter who wanted to know the truth. I was desperate. I was dying. Like George Bailey in *It's a Wonderful Life*, I wanted to live. Although a fictional character, everyone knew why George was on the bridge considering suicide. He was hopeless. He could not overcome his problem—and neither could I. But like George Bailey, I wanted to live.

The other steps would fall into place. I was now reading my Bible daily, attending AA meetings, and working the steps. I can remember reading my Bible one day and coming to a promise I knew was for me: "No temptation has seized you except what is common to man. And God is faithful; He will not let you be tempted beyond what you can bear. But when you are tempted, He will also provide a way out so that you can stand up under it" (1 Corinthians 10: 13).

I was still traveling as a salesman in the optical industry. I was coming out of a sales call in Kentucky when I had an overwhelming desire to take a drink. I had just celebrated thirty consecutive days of sobriety, of which I was very proud. Now came this desire, this craving, which I had never been able to overcome. Armed with this promise which I had memorized, I began to talk with my Higher Power, God. I talked to Him as if He were sitting in the car with me. I said, "God, you promised me you would not let me tempted beyond what I can bear. You promised me you would provide a way out so I could stand it. Well, you better do something or I am going to take a drink, and I do not want to take a drink. Please help me out of this." I talked and prayed for several minutes, all the time driving and making turns without paying attention to where I was going. I ended up lost in a subdivision. When I stopped, I realized there was no where I could get a drink. The urge had passed, and I had learned the power of praying God's promises to me back to Him.

When I got to my motel room, I called home and learned my grandmother had died. Early the next morning I started the journey home, but my car would not start. I pushed it to a filling station where we got it started, but the mechanic warned me not to turn it off or I would never get it started again. I prayed the same promise back to God, asking Him to make a way out of my predicament. I added, "Please get me back to Madison County." I drove from Bowling Green, Kentucky, down through Nashville where I got gas without turning off my engine. When I passed the sign telling me I was in Madison County, my car went dead! I got out laughing and crying at the same time. I was overwhelmed, and I now knew something about this God. I was, in fact, coming to know Him. I had obeyed the command, the YIELD sign, and as a result, I had not made the U TURN!

I decided I needed to get off the road and make it my priority to work the program and be home every night. I went to work for my in-laws in their music store, thinking it would be temporary as I looked for work that would pay more. I worked there for three years, and during that time, Gina and I had two sons, John and Ben. I did not return to the optical industry until 1980.

I was saved, sober, and sane. I had begun a new life and new way of living. I had a Guide who was going to direct me. He gave me a road map with sixty-six books.

LIFE IS DIFFICULT

So begins M. Scott Peck's classic book, *The Road Less Traveled.* "Life is difficult." Peck goes on to explain what each of us learns: life is a series of problems. We must learn to solve the problems. I could not solve this problem.

I remember reading an ad that seemed to be the solution to my problems. I needed to learn how to unleash the power within me, develop the will to win, and become stronger than I thought was possible. I bought the book to add to my growing library of self-help books. I wanted to be all of those things and do all of those things. If you had asked me what I was looking for, I would have handed you this book and said I wanted to unleash the power within me and become successful. If you had asked me where I was looking, I would have named the titles of these books, my resources which would take me to where I wanted to go. If you had asked me how it was working for me, I would have pointed to the fact I had a good job. But if you asked me what was holding me back, I would have had to confess my drinking was a problem. If you asked what I was doing about my drinking, I would have answered I am learning ways to unleash my subconscious mind to overcome the power of alcohol. And how was that working? It was not. Time was running out. Even more frightening, I was running out of hope.

On that September morning at my first AA meeting, I learned a truth that began the process of setting me free. The meeting started by reading the Twelve Steps. The first three were completely opposite of what I had spent years believing. It was not that these books did not contain principles and actions that were true; it was that they did not lead me to the only True and Living God who would become the Power within me and make these changes possible.

Here was what I heard in the first three steps that turned my life right side up:

1. We admitted we were powerless over alcohol and our lives had become unmanageable.
2. Came to believe that a Power greater than ourselves could restore us to sanity.
3. Made a decision to turn our will and our lives over to the care of God as we understood Him.

This is what I had just done that very morning in my hotel room. I was then led to my first AA meeting where this was reinforced and further followed up by a "good Samaritan" who took me to his office after the meeting and called my wife, Gina.

What was this Power within me that now could be unleashed? When I went down on my knees that morning, I went down as a sot. *Sot* is an old English word for a habitual drunkard. I had no power within me to overcome my addiction to alcohol, and it had set in action a chain of predictable events that led me to that morning of near death. When I arose from my knees, I arose as a saint. *Saint* is translated from a Greek word which means "set apart, sanctified." I was a different creature, for I now had within me the Holy Spirit. This Power within me began the process of guiding my life and supplying the ability to overcome my addiction to alcohol.

In theological language, I had experienced salvation. I had been born again of the Spirit. I was a new creature and old things would pass away and all things become new. I got saved. I began to get sober, sane, and in God's proper timing, successful.

Life continued to be difficult, but now I had within me the power to deal with difficulties. I first heard these truths almost thirty-eight years ago. I am now approaching seventy years of age. I have learned so much through these years of leaning on God Almighty. I have His Word as a lamp unto my feet to show me the way to steer through life's difficulties. I have His promise He will never place more on me than I can bear. He is my personal life coach. He is the way, the truth and the life. He will never leave me.

We all have within us a hunger for something. We want to get the most out of this life, yet sometimes the more things we get, the emptier we seem to become, ever learning but never coming to the truth. We climb the ladder of success only to reach the top, look back, and realize we had leaned our ladder against the wrong wall.

The apostles came to know life was difficult. The Apostle Paul's difficulties were many. Our forefathers who founded this country risked their lives to establish this nation. From the Pilgrims, who endured unbelievable hardships, to the framers of our constitution, who understood what it took to build a nation that would stand the tests of time, come these words that these wise men wrote and believed: "We hold these truths to be self-evident that all men are created equal, that they are endowed by their Creator with certain unalienable Rights, that among these are Life, Liberty and the pursuit of Happiness" (Declaration of Independence).

These men knew and believed there was a Creator. These men knew it was our Creator who gave us these desires for life, liberty and the pursuit of happiness. They also knew the One who gave you those desires was the only One who could satisfy those desires.

On July 28, 1787, James Madison recorded the following amazing address by eighty-one-year-old Benjamin Franklin at the Constitutional Convention. The convention was at a deadlock over the matter of congressional representation. Larger states wanted it based on population while smaller states wanted one vote per state. They were discovering that life was not only difficult, requiring sacrifice, but establishing a new way of governing was extremely difficult. Here are the words of wisdom from Franklin:

"In this situation of this Assembly, groping as it were in the dark to find political truth, and scarce able to distinguish it when presented to us, how has it happened, that we have not once thought of humbly applying to the Father of lights to illuminate our understanding? In the beginning of the contest [war] with Great Britain, when we were sensible of danger we had daily prayer in this room for divine protection. Our prayers were heard and they were graciously answered. All of us who were engaged in the struggle must have observed frequent instances of a superintending Providence in our favor. To that kind of providence we owe this happy opportunity of consulting in peace on the means of establishing our future felicity. And have we *now forgotten our Powerful Friend? Or do we imagine we no longer need His assistance?* I have lived a long time, and the longer I live, the more convincing proofs I see of this truth--**God governs in the affairs of men.** And if a sparrow cannot fall to the ground without His notice, is it probable that an empire cannot rise without His aid? We have been assured in the sacred writings that, 'except the Lord build the house, they labor in vain that build it.' I firmly believe this, and also believe, without His concurring aid, we shall succeed in this political building no better than the builders of Babel. We shall be divided by our little partial local interests; our projects will be confounded, and we ourselves shall become a reproach and bye word down to future ages. And what is worse, mankind may hereafter from this unfortunate instance, despair of establishing governments by human wisdom and leave it to chance, war, and conquest. I therefore beg leave to move that henceforth prayers imploring the assistance of Heaven, and its blessings on our deliberations, be held in this Assembly every morning before we proceed to business by one or more of the clergy of this city."[4]

I love this story! These men knew where to turn in difficult times—to Almighty God. The result was that their prayerful efforts were nothing less than the Constitution of the United States of America.

Like Franklin, the longer I live, the more convincing proofs I see of this truth that God governs in the affairs of men. To build and labor to satisfy one's basic desires without Him is to labor in vain. I had been groping in the darkness searching for the truth. I had been laboring in vain in attempting to build a life. It was not contained in those self-help books. I had been taught the right path to take by my parents, but I would not walk in it. Finally, I came to my senses and, like the prodigal, I turned around and headed for home to a loving, faithful Father, a powerful Friend, a very present help in the time of trouble.

Jesus told us we would have trouble in this world, but He told us to rejoice for He has overcome the world. Peter said don't even consider it strange when we encounter fiery trials. James said he rejoiced in tribulation. Once you accept life is difficult, you can start to look for the way to deal

---

[4] "The Debates in the Federal Conventions," 1781. Reported by James Madison, Oxford University Press, 1920.

with those difficulties. "Jesus said, 'I am the way'" (John 14:6).

At eighty-one years of age, Franklin was still seeing convincing proofs of the reality of God's involvement in the affairs of men. At seventy, I, too, continue to see convincing proofs of God's governing in the affairs of man.

Life is difficult. But since that day many years ago, I have had the power within me to deal with life's difficulties. I am learning each day how to unleash the power within me, the power of God Almighty. It lifted me up from a miry pit and set me on solid ground. Now I have been set free to pursue life, liberty, and happiness.

May I say to you, dear reader, you can have this power within you also. The Samaritan woman at the well had looked for something that would satisfy her life. She had looked for this satisfaction in relationships. She wanted someone to love, and someone to love her back. She had already been married five times and was currently living with a man who was not her husband. Jesus said to her: "If you knew the gift of God and who it is that asks you for a drink; you could have asked him and he would have given you living water" (John 4:10).

What is this gift of living water? It is the gift of salvation which provides forgiveness of one's sins, eternal life, and peace that passes understanding. Jesus is the one who controls this gift, this living water. It is yours for the asking when you are willing to repent and receive it.

Will you not ask Him? What are you waiting for? "If you confess with your mouth 'Jesus is Lord' and believe in your heart that God raised Him from the dead, you will be saved" (Romans 10:9). When He comes into your life, you will have within you the same power that raised Jesus from the dead. As you obey Him and follow Him, He will unleash this power in your life.

THE BEND IN THE ROAD

"But while he was still a long way off, his father saw him and was filled with compassion for him; he ran to his son, threw his arms around him and kissed him" (Luke 15:20).

In my imagination I see the father of the prodigal standing at the very place on his property where he last saw his son disappear around the bend in the road. This was a place he may have come to often, looking wistfully to that very bend and lifting up prayers for his lost son. As far as he knew, his son could be dead.

Then finally, oh glorious day, he looked and saw a familiar figure. His stooped posture looked as if he was carrying a weight upon his shoulders. His weariness spoke of a long and tiresome journey. He had no cart to carry his possessions; he only had what was on his back. But the father, filled with such joy and compassion, lifted his robes and began to run toward his son.

Now to understand this parable we must back up and see the situation that prompted the telling of this famous story and the audience who heard it on that long ago day.

"Now the tax collectors and sinners were all gathering around to hear him [Jesus]. But the

Pharisees and the teachers of the law muttered, 'This man welcomes sinners and eats with them.' Then Jesus told them a parable: 'Suppose one of you has a hundred sheep and loses one of them. Does he not leave the ninety-nine in the open country and go after the lost sheep until he finds it? And when he finds it, he joyfully puts it on his shoulders and goes home. Then he calls his friends and neighbors together and says, 'Rejoice with me; I have found my lost sheep.' I tell you that in the same way there will be more rejoicing in heaven over one sinner who repents than over ninety-nine righteous persons who need to repent."

"Or suppose a woman has ten silver coins and loses one. Does she not light a lamp, sweep the house and search carefully until she finds it? And when she finds it, she calls her friends and neighbors together and says, 'Rejoice with me; I have found my lost coin.' In the same way, I tell you, there is rejoicing in the presence of angels of God over one sinner who repents." (Luke 15:1-10).

This parable was told in response to the attitudes and the mutterings of the Pharisees and teachers of the law. These self-righteous hypocrites could not understand why Jesus would spend his time with sinners. Jesus shows us that God the Father's primary concern is the salvation of the lost. In doing so, Jesus reveals what takes place in heaven when one sinner repents. There is a celebration in heaven with much rejoicing in the presence of the angels of God over the repentance of one sinner.

THE JOURNEY OF THE PRODIGAL

The Good Shepherd came looking for me, to carry me back home. The Holy Spirit took the Word of God, a light upon my path and a lamp unto my feet, and guided me back home. I was swept clean, cleansed from my sins. This was the message Jesus was sending to the Pharisees and the teachers of the law. Jesus was telling them God the Father's priority was lost sinners. Jesus attracted sinners; He did not repel them. (I wonder if our churches today attract sinners or repel them.) Jesus understood sinners; He did not condemn them. This parable was encouraging to the sinners on that day, but it was offensive to the Pharisees and teachers who are represented by the self-righteous, works-oriented elder brother in the story.

"The son said to him, 'Father, I have sinned against heaven and you. I am no longer worthy to be called your son.' But the father said to his servants, 'Quick! Bring me the best robe and put it on him. Put a ring on his finger and sandals on his feet. Bring the fattened calf and kill it. Let's have a feast and celebrate. For this son of mine was dead and is alive again; he was lost and is found.' So they began to celebrate!"(Luke 15:21-24). Talk about a party--this was a celebration unlike any others.

In the Gospel of John, we have the first recorded miracle of Jesus. It takes place at a wedding in Cana of Galilee. The wine ran out, and Jesus' mother asked Him to intervene to solve the problem. Jesus then took the ceremonial water in the stone pots used for cleansing and changed it into wine.

Consider the remarks of the master of ceremonies: "Everyone brings out the choice wine first and then the cheaper wine after the guests have had their fill; but you have saved the best till now!" (John 2:10). This was a party, a celebration. Guess who was the life of the party? Jesus! He saves the best for last; He turns the water into wine. When I got saved and sober, the Lord turned the wine (alcohol) in my life into a new house. I took a job with my in-laws, making less money than before, but we had more than before because I had quit drinking.

Here is the before-and-after: I was dead but now was alive. I was lost but now was found. I was listening to the story of the prodigal son on a Wednesday night at Woodland Baptist Church. Ben Wilkes, our associate pastor, was preaching on the Prodigal Son. I realized this was my story. I also realized I needed to be baptized. The night I was baptized, my family was there. After the baptism, I told my mother I had wanted to get my baptism in order. She answered, "You didn't just get your baptism in order; you got saved!"

A few years later, I was relating my story to my pastor, Brother Bob Ervin. He listened until I was through, then he said, "I want you to share your testimony with the church this Sunday night." I agreed. After I got home and told my wife, she said, "Well, now you will have to tell your children." I had never told them about my battle with alcohol, and I must admit, I really did not want them to know how their daddy had been at one time. However, I knew what I must do.

Our daughter Carrie was around eleven; the boys, John and Ben, were nine and eight. They sat down on the twin beds in the boy's bedroom, and I told them my story. They were so still and so attentive—no squirming or interrupting me. They seemed to sense the importance of what I was telling them. When I was through, I asked them what they thought. I will never forget what Carrie said, "You have a neat testimony, Dad!" Do you have a testimony?

Brother Bob, like many preachers, liked alliteration, and he came up with one that I shall never forget. In the bulletin, he announced, "Come hear Tim Fortner's testimony Sunday night: 'From a Sot to a Saint.'" I couldn't have said it better myself. It became my story, my testimony: I was lost, but now am found. I was dead, but now I am alive. I was a sot; now I am a saint.

The prodigal had come home.

The Past, the Present and the Future

"But one thing I do: Forgetting what is behind and straining toward what is ahead, I press on toward the goal to win the prize for which God has called me heavenward in Christ Jesus" (Philippians 3:13).

I understand concentrating on one thing, the one thing that is most important. However, how does one forget?

I know we will forget some things with time, but there are other things we will always remember, both the good and significant as well as the bad and insignificant. How can I forget something when my mind will not let me, even though I want to forget it? Someone can tell you, "don't worry," but I am sure you have discovered those two words never seem to go together. Some things we cannot help worrying about. So how do we forget the unforgettable? We must put it in perspective, and we must see what the Word of God says.

"He [God] forgave us all our sins, having cancelled the written code, with its regulations, that was against us and that stood opposed to us; He took it away, nailing it to the cross. And having disarmed the powers and authorities, He made a public spectacle of them, triumphing over them by the cross" (Colossians 2: 14-15). Our past sins are under the blood. Nailed to the cross. He breaks the power of cancelled sin.

Did you notice how eager the prodigal's father was to forgive his son? He ran to him. This dignified, older man with two grown sons gathered up his robes and ran like an excited child to embrace his son. There was no one happier to see me come home than my Heavenly Father. I must not let my past influence my present and, thereby, alter my future. My future must dictate my present and put my past in perspective. I must be focused on the future like the runner focuses on the finish line. I will not look back. I will look to finish strong. In fact, I am headed for the finish line. I will not let my past be a shackle that keeps me from running the race set before me. I am drawing closer to the finish line of what started out as a marathon. Now, looking back, it seems more like a dash. The father of the prodigal had plans for his son who was dead but now alive, lost but now found. Our heavenly Father has plans for you and me also. Plans to prosper us. To be sure, the enemy and your old nature and this world we live in will cut in on your race. Keep your eyes on things above. Press on!

When I got saved and began to live sober, I somehow knew instinctively that I needed to stay at home and not travel. I had gained wisdom I did not possess before. I had to look at my present circumstances in light of my past experience and my future goals.

I developed a simple check list for decision making. I asked myself the following questions:

Is it helpful physically, mentally, and spiritually?

Does it have the ability to bring me under its power? Is it habit forming?

Will it hurt others?

Does it glorify God?

I had yielded. I had not made a U-turn at a moment of temptation. I have stumbled, and I will continue to stumble, but I will not be utterly cast down for the Lord upholds me with His right hand. I had finally come home. And there is no place like home.

THE WELCOME HOME CELEBRATION

"So they began to celebrate. Meanwhile, the older son was in the field. When he came near the house, he heard music and dancing. So he called one of the servants and asked him what was going on. 'Your brother has come,' he replied, 'and your father has killed the fattened calf because he has him back safe and sound.' The older brother became angry and refused to go in. So his father went out and pleaded with him. But he answered his father, 'Look! All these years I've been slaving for you and never disobeyed your orders. Yet you never gave me even a young goat so I could celebrate with my friends. But when this son of yours who has squandered your property with prostitutes comes home, you kill the fattened calf for him!' 'My son', the father said, 'You are always with me, and everything I have is yours. But we had to celebrate and be glad, because this brother of yours was dead and now is alive again; he was lost and is found" (Luke 15:24-32).

Now a personal disclaimer from your author: My older brother was not like the prodigal's older brother. In fact, at one time he came looking for me. I love my brother, Phil, and along with my sister,

Nancy, we have enjoyed and loved one another throughout our life's journey.

The elder brother in this parable is symbolic of the Pharisees. Notice how the elder brother spoke of his works and obedience to his father's rules. His father pleaded with him to come into the celebration, but it appears the elder brother would not. He stood outside, seething with envy which congealed into anger.

The repetition in these three mini-stories is clear: lost-found-rejoicing-celebration. Are you standing outside the celebration today? What is keeping you from going inside? Clearly you are invited.

One day in the future there will be a great celebration which Jesus compared to a great banquet in another parable. In that story, a certain man was preparing a great feast and invited many guests, we are told. We read the reasons people declined the invitation:

I have just bought a field. Building a business, seeking to make a name for yourself.

I just bought five yoke of oxen and I have to try them out. Possessions become our treasures.

I just got married. Relationships take precedent over our relationship with God.

This is the verdict: light has come into the world, but men prefer darkness, for their deeds are evil. A sinful lifestyle not turned from soon holds one in chains.

I will go back to an earlier question: What are you looking for in life? I had started out to celebrate life in riotous living, partying, and drinking just like the prodigal. My celebration of life was based on a lie. Only our Heavenly Father can provide us with the life worth celebrating. "The enemy comes to steal, kill and destroy, Jesus came that we might have life and have it more abundantly" (John 10:10).

Notice the word the elder brother used to describe his life, "All these years I've been slaving for you." Slaving does not sound like a life to be celebrated. What started out as fun for me—drinking and partying—soon became a cruel master, enslaving me and keeping me captive for fourteen years. The lie of the enemy is that sin provides a more fulfilling life than what God, Our Creator, can supply. Satan then reduces the risk to increase your interest. Watch the trap he set for Eve: "You will not surely die. For God knows that when you eat of it your eyes will be opened, and you will be like God" (Genesis 3:4-5). Do you see his method? Reduce the risk, thereby increasing the interest. The benefit is you will be like God. Both were lies, for Satan is the father of all lies.

What lie have you believed? When I set out to live life away from my parents' rules, I believed I could enjoy life more my way. The broad way looked a lot more exciting and fun than the narrow way. Besides that reasoning, everyone was going down the broad way. All the "cool" people were going in that direction. It took me ten years to realize I had gone the wrong way, and then it took me another four years before I could get turned around.

I discovered on September 16, 1977 the One for whom my heart had longed. I was lost, but was found by the Great Shepherd. He put me on His shoulder and carried me home where I belonged.

"Jesus answered, 'I am the way, the truth and the life. No one comes to the Father except through me'" (John 14:6).

Jesus is the life of the party! Come to the party! Come celebrate life!

THE SPIRITUAL DOMINO EFFECT

We are all aware of something we call the "domino effect." It is a metaphor used to describe a cascade of events which fall into place as a result of one certain action being taken. In 1983, a physicist at the University of British Columbia demonstrated the power of one domino to topple increasingly larger dominoes. Starting with a regular-sized domino, and having each domino one-and-a-half times larger, by the twenty-ninth domino you can theoretically topple a domino the size of the Empire State Building!

The domino effect can apply physically, mathematically, and politically. I also believe it applies spiritually. And since it does, I believe God created the domino effect. He only had to create the universe once. He only had to create the earth and everything in it, set it in space, and give it a spin. It has been spinning and reproducing ever since.

In Acts 17 we read of a most interesting encounter between Paul and the intellectual crowd in Athens. Paul used the altar to an "Unknown God" as the basis for his argument. He proclaimed, "Now what you worship as something unknown, I am going to proclaim to you" (vs. 23).

Today we are surrounded by a growing crowd of intellectuals who do not know God. He is unknown to them. Paul explained, "The God who made the world and everything in it is the Lord of heaven and earth and does not live in temples built by human hands" (vs. 24).

Paul continued, "From one man He made every nation of men, that they should inhabit the whole earth; and He determined the times set for them and the exact places they should live" (vs. 26). Paul explained the domino effect created by God when He created the world, in that every living thing He created contained the ability to reproduce after its own kind (Genesis 1:24). In doing so, God created the domino effect which has been falling into place ever since. Abraham became the "father of many nations" by the domino effect.

In Romans 5, Paul wrote: "You know the story of how Adam's sin landed us in the dilemma we're in: first sin, then death, and no one is exempt from either sin or death. That sin (Adam's) disturbed relations with God in everything and everyone, but the extent of this disturbance was not clear until God spelled it out for Moses."

"Here it is in a nutshell: Just as one person did it wrong and got us in all this trouble with sin and death, another person did it right and got us out of it. But more than just getting us out of trouble, He got us into life! One man said no to God and put many people in the wrong; one man (Jesus Christ) said yes to God and put many in the right" (Romans 5:12-14, 18-19, *The Message*).

Here we see the domino effect created by one person taking one action which led to a chain reaction—a cascade of events which fall into predictable place in ever increasing mathematical progression.

Paul understood this and knew there could be only one most important thing in his life which would impact every other area of his life. "*This one thing*" is an important phrase in the Christian's life or in any person's life for that matter. The rich young ruler who came to Jesus in Mark 10:21 wanted to know what he must do to inherit eternal life. "*One thing* you lack," [Jesus] said, "Go and sell everything you have and give it to the poor, and you will have treasure in heaven. Then come and follow me." We are told the rich young man went away sad because he had great wealth. He made his choice based on the one most important thing in his life, his wealth.

In Luke 10, Jesus was at the home of Lazarus, Martha, and Mary, enjoying fellowship with his friends. Martha was busy in the kitchen making preparations. Mary was sitting at the feet of Jesus listening to him. Martha was upset and felt it was unfair she should do all the work while Mary got to sit at His feet. "Tell her to help me!" she complained. "'Martha, Martha,' the Lord answered, 'you are worried and upset about many things, but only *one thing is* needed. Mary has chosen what is better, and it will not be taken away from her'" (Luke 10:41-42).

Again in Psalm 27:4, we read: *"One thing I have desired of the Lord, this is what I will seek that I might dwell in the house of the Lord all the days of my life."* Did you notice *the one thing* the writer desired is *the one thing* he sought? What are you seeking? Your answer will tell you what is most important in your life. It will direct your activities; it will consume your thoughts; it will direct your actions. It is the domino effect.

Cain was angry God did not accept his sacrifice but found favor with Abel's sacrifice. When God saw Cain's face was downcast, God asked Cain why he was upset. (God does not ask questions because He needs information; He asks questions to get us to look at ourselves.) God then explained how the domino effect worked: "If you do what is right, will you not be accepted? But if you do not do what is right, sin is crouching at your door; it desires to have you, but you must master it" (Genesis 4:6-7).

Time after time, God has explained in His Word, if you do this, then that will happen. If you do what is right, right things will come as a result. God tells us what actions will result in curses and what actions will result in blessings. God has "set before you life and death, blessings and curses. Now choose life, so that you and your children may live and that you may love the Lord your God, listen to His voice, and hold fast to Him. For the Lord is your life, and He will give you many years in the land He swore to your fathers, Abraham, Isaac and Jacob" (Deuteronomy 30: 19-20).

"Where your treasure is, there your heart will be also. No one can serve two masters. Either he will hate the one and love the other, or he will be devoted to the one and despise the other. You cannot serve God and Money" (Matthew 6:21, 24). Notice the word *devoted*. Devotion is connected to passion which drives you to acquire all that you desire.

My pursuit of happiness, enjoying life to the fullest, was devoted to drinking and partying as it is described in Luke 15—"wild living." The prodigal wasted his inheritance from his father, and so did I. Look at the domino effect in my life story. I left home in 1963, a seventeen-year-old in pursuit of the wild life. The first thing in my life was to have fun drinking and partying. When I put that first domino into action, it created all the rest of the dominoes that fell into place for the next fourteen years. Here are just a few of those dominoes: expelled from college four times in five years, married and divorced, an absentee father, a drunkard, an alcoholic, a heart-ache to my parents, a disappointment to myself and, finally, looking back, I saw nothing to look forward to but more of the same. I wanted to die and came close to committing suicide.

Then came that fateful day in September. What happened? At first I thought quitting drinking was the most important thing in my life, my biggest problem. But my problem was just a symptom. I discovered my problem could only be resolved by a Higher Power. I came to believe a Power greater than myself could restore me to sanity. I made a decision to turn my life and my will over to God as I understood Him.

As I began to understand God, I realized my problem was not my problem. My problem had been my priority. In Matthew 6:33, Jesus told us to "seek first the kingdom of God and His Righteousness." Put first things first. This then became my priority. When I put Him first, things begin to fall into place, just as He promised they would. "Seek first [God's] kingdom and His righteousness, and all these things will be given to you as well. Therefore do not worry about tomorrow, for tomorrow will worry about itself. Each day has enough trouble of its own" (Matthew 6:33-34). I now had placed into action the right thing. And when the domino you put in place is the right thing, then everything that falls into place will be the right thing.

Watch what happened: I went to work for my in-laws for minimum wage plus commission. I spent the next three years at home every night. While attending church and AA meetings, I became grounded in the Word and was able to build on the sobriety my Higher Power had enabled me to enjoy. We bought our first home together. Our family grew, and we had two sons to go with our daughter.

In 1980 I returned to the optical industry, and I began to experience success. In the early 1980s, my company brought in a national speaker for our accounts. What I saw and heard from that speaker awakened a desire in me to become a national speaker and trainer. I told my wife the night I came home from the meeting that I had seen what I wanted to be. Over the next thirty-five years, I became vice president of a major business. I was given the opportunity to test-market a product which became a global product. Then, in 1990, I went to work for Transitions Optical, a startup company with zero sales. I became their national speaker and, for twenty-one of the next twenty-five years, I spoke to more than 100,000 people on six continents. I also had the opportunity to be an adjunct professor at a professional school for four years.

In 1989 I began to teach a Bible class each Sunday, and I have continued teaching ever since. In 2014, the company I helped start was sold; it was valued at 3.4 billion dollars.

Here is what I have to say about this amazing life: "Now to Him who is able to do immeasurably more than all we ask or imagine, according to His power that is at work within us, to Him be glory in the church and in Christ Jesus throughout all generations, forever and ever. Amen" (Ephesians 3:20-21). There it is—the power within us, the power unleashed by faith can do more than we ever imagined. For surely I could not have ever imagined a life such as this. Did you see the domino effect? "Through all generations, forever and ever." It keeps on falling into place, toppling those things we could never have overcome.

This does not mean we will not have troubling circumstances in our lives. My parents died in their sixties within two years of each other. I was diagnosed with cancer. Both of our sons caused us sleepless nights with their wrong choices. Our daughter suffered a miscarriage, but later was blessed with twins. I had business ventures that brought me to the brink of bankruptcy. And recently my beloved wife, Gina, was diagnosed with ovarian cancer. In it all and through it all, we learned the process of how to keep "the main thing the main thing," as my good friend and former pastor, Charlie Martin, used to tell us every Sunday.

I did not and do not always do the right thing. When we get saved, our position is one of perfection, for we have the righteousness and holiness of Christ Jesus Himself. Unfortunately, our practice does not match our position. We fall short. We stumble. But we are not utterly cast down, for He holds us with His right hand.

I tried social drinking in the 1980s, but the results were the same. I could not drink alcohol and have not had a drink since. I was deceived into thinking I had come to a place in my maturity where I could drink and not get drunk. Paul warned us, "If you think you are standing firm, be careful that you don't fall" (1 Corinthians 10:12).

So, have you discovered what is the main thing in life? "This is eternal life, that they might know You, the True and Living God, and Jesus Christ, Whom you have sent" (John 17:3). This is why Paul counted everything else rubbish compared to knowing Christ.

The Westminster Catechism asks this question and offers this answer:

Q. What is the chief end of man?

A. Man's chief end is to glorify God and enjoy Him forever

The chief end is the main thing, to glorify God and enjoy Him forever. This is the one thing we must do.

What is the secret to life? Warren Wiersbe wrote a great little book entitled, _Five Secrets of Living_.[5] I strongly recommend you read this book. Here are the five secrets:

- The secret of living is fruit-bearing.
- The secret of fruit-bearing is abiding.
- The secret of abiding is obeying.
- The secret of obeying is loving.
- The secret of loving is knowing.

The main thing is to keep the main thing, the main thing.

"Seek first [God's] kingdom and His righteousness and all these things will be given to you" (Matthew 6:33). This is the One Thing we must do. Everything will fall into place—the power of the domino effect. The ability to overcome problems that once loomed over your life like Mount Everest can be toppled in the right sequence.

The domino effect is a mathematical progression which means it falls into a predictable sequence. Life from the time a sperm fertilizes an

---

[5] Living Books of Tyndale House Publishers, Inc.

egg develops in a sequence. Life is sequential. What we choose to make the most important thing in our life defines us.

The Twelfth Step of the Twelve Steps of AA reads as follows: "Having had a spiritual awakening as a result of these steps, we tried to carry this message to others, and to practice the principles in all our affairs."

In writing my story I want nothing more than to carry this message to others.

THE ROAD TO
NOWHERE

"If you don't know where you are going, any road
will take you there." (Anonymous)

A recent report from the Pew Research
Center entitled, "America's Changing Religious
Landscape" reveals America is a significantly less
Christian nation than it was seven years ago.[6] "This
trend is big, it's broad, and it's everywhere," said
Alan Cooperman, Pew's director of research.
"Christian faiths are troubled by generational
change. Each successive group is less concerned than
their parents."

When asked to identify their faith or religious
beliefs with conventional religious faiths and
denominations, many identify themselves as, "none
of the above." The "nones" are the new major force
in American faith. They are more secular in their
outlook and comfortable with admitting it. Atheists
and agnostics have doubled their share of the overall
marketplace.

---

[6] *USA Today*, May 15, 2015.

Where are they going? TO RELIGIOUS NOWHERE.[7]

How did we get here? We took a road that was well traveled, the broad way with the hard-packed earth where the seed, the Word of God, bounced off. Its gate was wide and the way was easy and many entered in there. Today many are not choosing to take the road less traveled, the narrow way, the strait gate. People complain the narrow way is too restrictive and confining; the broad way is more popular now than ever before. There is a principle in paths. A path leads to a specific destination. Unless one turns around and corrects his direction, the result is inevitable. Do you know where the broad way leads? It leads to destruction. Are you traveling down that path? Stop and turn around. The broad way comes to a dead end, literally and physically. I chose the broad way, and as a result I spent fourteen years on the destructive path. I realized early on the problems I was encountering, but I could not seem to accept they were a result of the direction I had chosen.

What was I seeking? I was seeking to have a good life, a life of fun and enjoyment. Where was I looking? I was looking on the broad way. All the signs, advertising, and word-of-mouth advice said this was where the good times were, this was the life you deserved, you only go around once, so live it up,

---

[7] *USA Today*, May 15, 2015. "Report: Country Less Christian."

enjoy life to the fullest. What had I found? Addiction. Destructive behavior. Heartache. Depression and despair. What did I do about it? I came to believe there was a Higher Power who could do for me and through me what I could not do in my own strength.

I have written this story for the following reasons:

- To leave a legacy for my children, grandchildren and great-grandchildren to come
- To tell my story as a warning to prodigals who are headed the wrong way.
- To let them know there is One who can truly help them. He did it for me and has for many others.
- To encourage those who love prodigals and let them know there is hope.
- Also, to encourage those of you who are boomers to write your own story and give your family something they will treasure for generations to come. It will be a gift that keeps on giving. Can you imagine if your parents, grandparents, or even great grandparents had left you such a legacy? It is a gift which can keep on giving for generations to come, a treasured family heirloom.
- For the Peabody Class of 1963, Trenton, Tennessee: you were a significant part of my journey. I have enjoyed all our reunions, and I

hope to see you at the best reunion ever—when we all get to heaven. When they call roll up yonder, will you be there? I pray you will.

"But these are written that you may believe that Jesus is the Christ, the Son of God, and that by believing you might have life in His Name."
(John 20:31)

A New Song in My Heart

"I waited patiently for the Lord; He turned to me and heard my cry. He lifted me out of the slimy pit, out of the mud and mire; He set my feet on a rock and gave me a firm place to stand. He put a new song in my heart, a hymn of praise to our God. Many will see and fear and put their trust in the Lord" (Psalm 40:1-3).

This is one of my wife's favorite Psalms. Gina has even more reason to claim this during this season of her life and ours as she is undergoing treatment for ovarian cancer. We both have come to understand God's ways are higher than our ways. He is too wise to be mistaken and too good to be unkind, as one popular song tells us. Our Heavenly Father always does what will provide the best possible results for the most people by the best possible means for the longest period of time.

God sometimes takes us to a place where we can get a clearer view of Him. Sometimes it is the pit of physical sickness, as Gina is now experiencing. All of a sudden the priorities of life change in an instant with one word—cancer.

We believe this is something God has allowed for our good and His glory. God allows us to endure the suffering for the joy set before us. He puts a new song in our hearts, a song of praise for our Heavenly Father who always knows what is best. The dark background of her illness and the quietness it brings serve to make the song ring with even more clarity and beauty. "Praise God from Whom all blessings flow; praise Him all creatures here below!"

I have been suffering from hearing loss for the last several years. Two years ago my hearing left me while I was speaking to a group, and I was, for all practical purposes, deaf. I qualified for a cochlear implant and received an implant about sixteen months ago. The improvement has been a blessing. However, I can no longer distinguish the tune or melody of music. It is only noise to me. I miss this part of my life as well as this part of my worship experience. It has caused me to focus on lyrics.

As I look back at the music of our times and why we liked it, I realize it was not only because "it had a good beat and you could dance to it,"[8] but also because musicians are the poets and philosophers of each time and age. They express everything from the thrill of love to the heartache of love not returned. They also express outrage against injustice, war, crime, and abuse.

The intellectual agnostics of our time and culture tell us God is no longer necessary and we have outgrown the need for religion and the myths of the Bible. Yet the words of today's music seem to

---

[8] American Bandstand's most common pronouncement on a new song.

say something entirely different. Whether it is songs which glorify sex, drugs, and violence or those which express the heartaches of life, one thing is obvious: From generation to generation the search for meaning in life goes on and on.

We are told we live in an enlightened era. The intellectual agnostics and collegiate professors—and, of course, Hollywood—tell us no longer are we to consider God relevant. And, if we do find it necessary to have a faith or religion, one belief system is recognized as good as the other. Christians should not be so prideful and bigoted as to believe their religion was the only one that counts. "We have outgrown the myths of the Bible," the elite educators tell their students. However, not only the songs of this era but the twenty-four-hour news cycle tell us the search for meaning is worldwide and universal. I believe we live in more fearful times than ever before, and the yearning for someone or something to bring peace has never been greater.

As I said earlier, lyrics have more significance to me since I cannot hear the melody of haunting violins, the riffs of the guitarist, or the fluid flow of the pianist. So I read the lyrics and also think about the songs of my era and wonder what the artists were trying to tell us.

I wonder if the words were an expression of the heart of the writer in search of something he or she could not seem to find. The Rolling Stones' biggest hit, "(I Can't Get No) Satisfaction," seemed to be the anthem of a teenager's coming of age. We were, after all, driving around in our cars and trying to be cool and figure it out. We tried what the advertisers said would give our life meaning, but satisfaction eluded us.

Another popular song, "Only Love Can Break a Heart" contained this truth: "Only love can break a heart, and only love can mend it again."

The Beatles, one of my all-time favorite groups, longed for yesterday when troubles seemed so far away. We can certainly agree with that sentiment. These same British young men also seemed to realize, as we all do sooner or later, we need help. We need somebody to be there for us, someone we can depend on through the years.

As I recall the lyrics of some of rock and roll's earliest artists, I muse about their motivation. For example, whose love was Jackie Wilson talking about that kept lifting him higher?

Burt Bacharach had his share of hits also. His lyrics seemed simple, but they make me think he expressed something about our needs. He told us all the things we did not need any more of, then told us what the world needs now is love—not just any kind of love—"but love, sweet love… the only thing there is just too little of."

Do you notice a theme? Love.

Jesus was once asked, "What is the greatest commandment?" What did He answer? "Love the Lord your God with all your heart and with all your soul and with all your mind… and the second is like it: Love your neighbor as yourself" (Matthew 22:37-39).

"On these two commandments," He said, "all of the Bible rested."

We live in a society that describes love in so many ways: we love our cars, boats, houses, clothes, hobbies, sports, money, work, etc. Can any of these things love you back? Of course not. Can money buy you love? Even the Beatles knew the answer to that one.

I will never forget watching a football game with my two sons when they were much younger. One of my boys asked me, "Which team are we for, Daddy?" When I told them who I was for, that became who they were for. Wow! How influential our examples are. It also reminds me of the awesome responsibility to show our loved ones and the world around us what real love looks like.

"For God so loved the world He gave..."

Do you give your love unconditionally?

What's love got to do with it? Everything!

God has put so many new songs in my heart. John Newton's classic, "Amazing Grace, "tells his story and the story of every prodigal: "Amazing grace how sweet the sound that saved a wretch like me! I once was lost, but now am found. Was blind but now I see." Or this classic hymn I have heard since my childhood: "I was sinking deep in sin, far from the peaceful shore, very deeply stained within, sinking to rise no more, but the Master of the sea, heard my despairing cry, from the waters lifted me, now safe am I. Love lifted me, Love lifted me, when nothing else could help, Love lifted me."[9]

It lifted me that day when, I was sinking to rise no more. And it keeps lifting me higher and higher each day, years later. I wonder, do any of these songs or lyrics resonate with the emptiness in your heart? Do you feel far from the peaceful shore? Are you sinking and feel like you are not going to be able to rise any more? Have you tried and tried but cannot find any satisfaction?

Then cry out to God, and He will lift you out of that miry pit, set you on solid rock, and put a new song in your heart.

Simply pray a prayer something like this: Lord Jesus, I realize I am a sinner. Sin has taken me further than I intended to go, cost me more than I wanted to pay, and kept me longer than I wanted to stay. I want to come home. I want to return to my Heavenly Father. I sinned against you. I repent of my sins; please forgive me. Amen.

Your Heavenly Father who has been waiting on you all your life has opened His arms wide for you, and all of heaven is rejoicing for the prodigal has returned home!

"Come to me," He says, "all who are weary and heavy laden. Come home."

There's no place like home.

My prayer as I end this book is that you will be encouraged to follow the Lord.

---

[9] "Love Lifted Me," lyrics by James Rowe.

THE CLASS OF 1963

Peabody High School

Many of my classmates from the class of 1963 I knew from kindergarten to graduation.

I would love to sit outside on those steps at old PHS one more time, waiting for the bell to ring, and tell you how much you meant to me—especially at our ten-year reunion—when I was so lost.

You helped me realize what a foolish young man I had become and made me want to be more like you.

God bless each one of you. Take a walk down memory lane with me and remember:

"The Way We Were"

Senior Class Officers

President	Jimmy Milligan
Vice-president	Lynn(Lefty) Harpole
Secretary and Treasurer	Ann Pinckley
Valedictorian	Betty Ingram
Salutatorian	Fred Oster
Third Highest	Lynn Fann

TIM FORTNER

WHO'S WHO

Best Personality	Robbie May
Best Personality	Mac Anderson
Most Studious	Betty Ingram
Most Studious	Lynn Fann
Best All Round	Ann Pinckley
Best All Round	Mac Anderson
Most Beautiful	Deloria Burkett
Most Handsome	Mac Anderson
Best Dressed	Kay Alexander
Best Dressed	Mac Anderson
Most Likely to Succeed	Andrea Jonas
Most Likely to Succeed	Fred Oster
Quietest Girl	Patsy Cude
Quietest Boy	Jim Baker
Cutest Girl	Kay Alexander
Cutest Boy	Lefty Harpole
Most Conscientious Girl	Betty Ingram
Most Conscientious Boy	Fred Oster
Best Athlete Girl	Ann Pinckley
Best Athlete Boy	Richie Flowers
Biggest Flirt Girl	Molly Milligan
Biggest Flirt Boy	Tommy Hadley
Most Original Girl	Andrea Jonas
Most Original Boy	Tim Fortner

SENIOR PLAY: *The Seventeenth Summer*

MUSIC, MOVIES AND TELEVISION

MUSIC:

"Big Girls Don't Cry"
"Breaking up is Hard to Do"
"Duke of Earl"
"Good Luck Charm"
"He's a Rebel"
"I Can't Stop Loving You"
"Surf City"
"Walk Like a Man"
"It's My Party"
"Blue Velvet"
"If You Wanna Be Happy"

MOVIES:

Lawrence of Arabia
To Kill a Mockingbird
Dr. No.
Cape Fear
The Birds
The Great Escape

TELEVISION:

The Beverly Hillbillies
Candid Camera
Red Skelton
Bonanza
The Lucy Show
The Dick Van Dyke Show
Gunsmoke

Have Gun Will Travel
Ben Casey
Andy Griffin Show
Rawhide
Perry Mason
Wagon Train
My Three Sons

PRICES:

Movie ticket	$1.25
Gasoline	29¢ per gallon
New House	$12,000
Average Salary	$6,000

We had no cell phones or personal computers in 1963. Television consisted of three channels and went off at midnight. Today we have larger houses but smaller families. We have more conveniences, but less time. We have more than 300 channels on high definition televisions but nothing worth watching.

We have multiplied our possessions but reduced our values. We have more experts and expertise, but our problems are greater than ever. We have more knowledge, ever learning, but never coming to the truth.

Perhaps you, or a loved one, are at a crossroads today. Are you looking for direction? Maybe when you read those questions to see if you had a problem with alcohol, your responses confirmed what you already knew—you have a problem with drinking. Contact Alcoholics Anonymous. They can get you on the road to sobriety, and you can begin with a decision to turn your will and life over to the care of God. Get in a Bible believing church and in a small group for Bible study.

Or you may have a prodigal you love dearly, and you are waiting, watching, and praying he or she will return. Charles Stanley says to fight all your battles on your knees in prayer. I cannot begin to imagine the prayers that went up for me from my mother and daddy, grandparents, and so many others. Keep on praying.

Jesus said, "I am the Way, the Truth, and the Life." Have you found the way? Discovered the truth? Found the life you were created to live? Pick up a copy of the best-selling book ever written, the Bible. It is life-giving, life-transforming, and life-sustaining. It is a map that leads you to the greatest treasures ever imagined!

I know because on September 16, 1977, at the point of suicide, *I went down on my knees a sot, and I came up a Saint!*

THE REST OF THE STORY

If you have come this far with me on my journey, let us return to the original story of the Prodigal Son and the end of his journey. I have read the story many, many times. I have also read numerous commentaries on this subject.

In his book, *The Prodigal God: Recovering the Heart of the Christian Faith*, Pastor Timothy Keller provided me with a rich insight into this story. His use of the word, *recovering*, in his title resonated with me as I am a *recovering alcoholic*. In fact my first AA meeting was in the basement of a church in Nashville, TN. A church which opened its doors to people like myself where we might begin the recovery process and develop a relationship with our Higher Power.

I am so grateful to Dr. Keller for sharing his insight and getting me to think anew about a story I thought I knew so well. Let me share with you what he brought to my attention and also encourage you to read his book.

If you are familiar with this parable I would like to invite you to imagine you are in the crowd on that day Jesus spoke and hear this parable as if for the first time. We are told, from previous passages, that Jesus is attracting large crowds to hear him speak. Jesus was, and is, the master teacher of all times. His story telling provided his audiences with easy to remember stories, yet lifted their thoughts to puzzle over their deeper meanings. Jesus got their attention and more importantly he got them to think.

The passage opens by describing the audience on this day. "Now the tax collectors and sinners were all gathering around to hear him. But the Pharisees and the teachers of the law muttered, 'This man welcomes sinners and eats with them'" (Luke15:1, 2). To eat with a person in this culture was to recognize them as your equal.

If you were there that day, you would have recognized the difference by their dress and attitude. The Pharisees wore their religion on their sleeves, literally. Their religious garb identified them. Their attitude of superiority would have been easily detected in their body language and the words they spoke. One could not help but notice as Jesus taught the frowns on their faces, the anger, the muttering, and the smugness of their pride.

Here is my first question for you: with whom would you be sitting with on that day? The tax collectors and sinners would be considered the outsiders and the Pharisees would be considered the insiders. The Pharisees were the elite members of the Sanhedrin, the most influential group in all of Israel. They were the ultimate insiders. These were the 'movers and shakers', the in-crowd. They were educated, prosperous, pompous, prideful and self-righteous. This Jesus and his teaching and association with tax collectors and sinners was an affront to them.

Now listen to the story as if for the first time and notice what is obviously missing in the third part of the three-part story. First narrative is straightforward, a shepherd with 100 sheep loses one of them. He leaves the 99 to go and find the one lost sheep. He joyfully puts the lost sheep on his shoulders and goes home. He calls his friends and neighbors and invites them to rejoice with him over the finding of the one lost sheep. Jesus then tells the audience in the same way there will be more rejoicing in heaven over the one sinner who repents than the 99 righteous persons who do not need to repent.

Second story involves a woman who has ten silver coins and loses one. She lights a lamp, sweeps the house and searches carefully until she finds it. Like the first story, she calls her friends and neighbors to rejoice with her for she has found the lost coin. Again Jesus tells the multitude, in the same way there is rejoicing in heaven in the presence of angels before God over one sinner who repents.

The third story unfolds. "There was a man who had two sons." The younger son asked his father for his share of the estate. According to custom, the elder brother would receive a double portion. The father granted his request and divided the property between them. The younger son gets $1/3^{rd}$ of the estate, the elder brother the remaining 2/3rd's. The father has given up everything.

We read of the younger son's lifestyle and how he ends up squandering his inheritance. Ending up broke in the far country, the younger son is destitute. A severe famine makes his life even more difficult, and he ends up with a job feeding pigs.

The audience hearing this for the first time, must be anticipating someone coming to search for the lost son. This has been the pattern of the parable. The absence of a rescuer makes one wonder why no one came. Who should have come?

We then read the prodigal son comes to his senses and realizes what has happened to him. He heads for home. His father sees him from a long way off and runs to meet his son. The prodigal cannot even get his rehearsed speech of repentance out for his father hugging and kissing him. The father immediately calls his servants. He is so excited. "Quick! Bring the best robe and put a ring on his finger and sandals on his feet. And bring the fattened calf here and kill it and let us eat and be merry; for this is my son who was dead and is alive again; he was lost and found." (Luke 15:22-24) So they began to celebrate.

The elder brother hears the music, and asks one of the servants what is going on? Your brother has come home and your father has killed the fattened calf because he is back safe and sound. The elder brother becomes angry and refuses to go into the celebration.

THE JOURNEY OF THE PRODIGAL

His father went out and pleaded with him to come into the celebration. The angry elder brother answered his father: "Look! All these years I've been slaving for you and never disobeyed your orders. Yet you never gave me even a young goat so I could celebrate with my friends. But when this son of yours who has squandered your property with prostitutes comes home, you kill the fattened calf for him." (Luke 15:28-30)

"My son," the father said to him, "you are always with me and everything I have is yours. But we must celebrate and be glad because this brother of yours was dead and is now alive again; he was lost and is found."

Now who do you suppose the tax collectors and sinners identified with—the prodigal son or the younger brother? They identified with the prodigal son and the Pharisees identified with the elder brother.

The elder brother should have come to his father and volunteered to go to the far country to find his younger brother and bring him back to his father. It was his duty. He was his brother's keeper. He should have been willing to go at his own expense and tell his father, "I will use all you have given me to finance the journey and rescue my brother—lest he perish."

The father in the parable represents our Heavenly Father. The sons were both wrong, both lost. Pastor Keller describes the heart of the Gospel this way. Everyone is loved. Everyone is wrong.

Everyone needs to recognize they are wrong. Everyone needs to change by placing their faith in Jesus Christ. The father loved both sons. The father went out to meet the returning prodigal and also he went out in the field to his elder son to plead with him to come in and join the celebration.

Jesus told this parable in response to the Pharisee's criticism regarding his association with tax collectors and sinners. The story was primarily for the Pharisees and teachers of the law. The tax collectors and sinners were blessed and overjoyed with the acceptance of the prodigal son. The tax collectors knew what it was to be despised by their own people. Yet Jesus invited one tax collector named Levi to be one of his original disciples. We know him better as Matthew.

When the father told the elder son, "everything I have is yours," he was stating a fact. He had divided the estate between his two sons. The younger son had spent it all. All that he had left belonged to the elder brother. The elder brother did not want to spend it on the younger son. The robe, the ring, the sandals, the fattened calf were actually his possessions. He did not want to be his brother's keeper. *Forgiveness always involves a price. The elder brother in this parable did not want to pay it.*

The father in the parable went to both sons. He is the one who initiated the contact. This is our Heavenly Father. He is not willing that any should perish but all would come to repentance. He loved the prodigal and he loved the elder son. Jesus loves

THE JOURNEY OF THE PRODICAL

sinners. Our Heavenly Father's main concern is to see lost souls saved. His second greatest concern is to see saved people as concerned about the lost as He is. Perhaps as you consider this parable you find yourself identifying with the younger brother, the tax collectors and sinners, for all have sinned. However, sometimes you find yourself acting like the elder brother and the Pharisees, pointing out the sins of others with unforgiveness in your heart.

Dr. Keller goes on to explain who our True Elder Brother is. The Lord Jesus is our True Elder Brother. Everything the Father has, He has given to the Son. The Son volunteered to leave his home in heaven and give up everything to come to the far country and bring his younger brothers and sisters home to the great joy of His Father. It cost Him everything, His very life.

I encourage anyone to read all four of the Gospels and then tell me what you find wrong with Jesus. Pilate said he could find no fault in the man. He is perfect. He is the epitome of kindness. Notice in every encounter with an outsider and a Pharisee, Jesus was always on the side of the outsider. In John 4, Jesus encounters a Samaritan woman at a well. She has been married five times and is currently living with a man, not her husband. Jesus initiates contact with her. Jesus crosses all types of boundaries—sexual, gender, economic, age, racial—and reaches out to sinners of all types. Read the fascinating account in Luke 7 of Jesus eating with a Pharisee named Simon when a prostitute comes in and anoints his feet while he is eating. Simon condemns the woman and Jesus for allowing her to anoint his feet. Jesus rebukes Simon and sides with the woman. All through the Gospel you will find Jesus reaching out to all kinds of sinners, including the Pharisees and Roman soldiers. He loved them all, and longed to gather them to himself as a mother hen would her chicks. But sadly many would not.

Want to get a picture of what Jesus expects of us as Christians? Read Matthew 25, and read who He welcomes into His kingdom: "Come, you who are blessed by my Father, take your inheritance, the kingdom prepared for you since the creation of the world. For I was hungry and you gave me something to eat, I was thirsty and you gave me something to drink, I was a stranger and you invited me in, I needed clothes and you clothed me, I was sick and you looked in on me, I was in prison and you came and visited me." Then the righteous answered, "When did we see you hungry and feed you, or thirsty and give you something to drink? When did we see you a stranger and invite you in, or needing clothes and clothe you? When did we see you sick and look in on you or go to prison and visit you?"

"The King will reply, 'I tell you the truth, whenever you did this for *the least of my brothers of mine, you did for me'*" (Matthew 25). The *least* of my brothers. Jesus is our True Elder Brother.

I remember my first AA meeting was in the basement of a church in Nashville, TN. When I started attending AA meetings in Jackson, my hometown, the group I came to join met in the basement of a church. Our meetings had but one purpose—to help and encourage one another to stay sober one day at a time. To help one another work the 12 Steps of Recovery and establish our relationship with our Higher Power by discovering the recovery process. In any and every AA meeting I ever attended, there was a wide variety of people. Male, female, young, old and in-between. Different races, different backgrounds. All kinds of economic backgrounds, occupations and past history. We welcomed all.

Wouldn't it be wonderful if our churches looked like AA meetings? Where people realized we are all recovering sinners. Trying to stay on the right path one day at a time and helping others discover the way of recovery through a relationship to their Heavenly Father through His Son, our True Elder Brother, and Jesus Christ.

How do you think the prodigal son looked that day? Smelled? I know he was hungry and thirsty. He was in need of clothes. He had been a stranger in a foreign country, would he be one in his own home? You could smell him ten feet away. Hear the congestion in his lungs with each wracking cough? He needs medical attention. What do you bet the prodigal had seen his share of nights inside a jail?

Now look around your church today. Are the outsiders, the prodigals, welcome there? Or does the hymn, "Just as I Am" really mean you are surrounded by people just as you are? Are we attracting sinners or repelling them? Does your light shine in the darkness or is it put under the shade of the inside walls of a pristine church building?

For you see, recovery is the heart of the Gospel. It is a rescue mission. We are all recovering from sin, to which we were all addicted. Jesus said when you did it to the least of these my brothers—you did it for me.

At some point in your life you realize you were born into God's story. My life story was written before I was ever born. It included my parents and how they came to meet, got married and had a family. Paul explained this to the men of Athens in Acts 17, telling us we were born in the exact time and place God willed for us to be born. We entered God's story. And God has told us He knows the story He has for us—the life He intends for us to live. I have shared my story just as others have shared their story that we might identify with them—being encouraged. It is amazing the success which Alcoholics Anonymous has experienced in helping others achieve: long term sobriety, changed lives and families restored and reconciled. How did they accomplish this miracle? By sharing their stories. Stories have power. The Bible is God's story. It allows us to see ourselves in the characters of the Bible. It tells us where we came from, why we are here and where we are headed.

"Is life a tale told by an idiot, full of sound and fury, signifying nothing," as Macbeth opined? I submit to you, if you have not figured out God is the author of life and the author and perfecter of our faith, you are trapped in a tale of self-discovery. A story which has taken you on the broad way in search of meaning. Your story is not going to end well. Here is the bottom line: without God, life is meaningless. You cannot figure out the story.

Stories are how we figure out things. Stories are the language of the heart. All of life is a story. Have you discovered the endless story you were born into?

"Tell me not in mournful number life is but an empty dream! For the soul is dead that slumbers and things are not what they seem. Life is real! Life is earnest! And the grave is not the goal; dust thou art, to dust returneth, was not spoken of the soul. Lives of great men all remind us we can make our lives sublime. And departing, leave behind us footprints in the sand of time. Footprints that, perhaps, another sailing o'er life's solemn main, a forlorn and shipwrecked brother, seeing, shall take heart again. Let us, then, be up and doing with a heart for any fate; still achieving, still pursuing, learn to labor and wait."[10]

Longfellow knew our life stories have the ability to encourage others.

What are you leaving behind? We each have a story to tell. A legacy for our families and encouragement for others. God's story finds its way into every story we encounter, whether it be a

---

[10] Henry Wadsworth Longfellow.

movie, a novel or a story we are following on the news. It is the age-old story of love and hate, of hardships and blessings. The stories of trial and error, intrigue and mystery, loyalty and betrayal, good and evil.

Now that you know the power of a story, perhaps you understand why I have written mine. Everyone has a story. And everyone has someone who would be interested in their story. My question to you is, "What is your story?"

ABOUT THE AUTHOR

Tim Fortner and his wife, Gina, reside in Jackson, TN. They have three children and two grandchildren. They are members of West Jackson Baptist Church. Tim has been a Bible teacher for the last 26 years. He has told his story, "From a Sot to a Saint," to hundreds of people throughout the years.

Mr. Fortner has spent more than 40 years in the optical industry. He played a major role in the development of a new technology in plastic photochromic lenses for PPG. In 1990 following his involvement in the test market, Tim joined the new start-up company, Transitions Optical. He would spend the next 20 plus years helping to build a global brand. As an international speaker for Transitions Optical, Tim has spoken to more than 100,000 eye care professionals worldwide.

Today, Tim is the CEO and founder of the Fortner Consulting Group and continues to provide continuing education to eye care professionals, primarily in the USA and Canada.

He teaches a weekly Bible study class. Tim is also available for speaking engagements.

You may contact Tim @ johntfortner@gmail.com

Made in the USA
Columbia, SC
25 August 2021